THE
ROBBER
BRIDEGROOM

Book and Lyrics by Alfred Uhry
Music by Robert Waldman
Based on the novella by Eudora Welty

DRAMA BOOK SPECIALISTS (PUBLISHERS)
NEW YORK

Library of Congress Cataloging in Publication Data
Waldman, Robert.
    The robber bridegroom.
    1. Musical revues, comedies, etc.—Librettos. I. Uhry, Alfred. The robber bridegroom. II. Title.
ML50.W1537R6 1978   782.8'1'54   78-16996
ISBN 0-89676-001-4 Cloth
ISBN 0-89676-006-5 Paper

10 9 8 7 6 5 4 3 2 1

Manufactured in the United States of America

For J., who always tells me the truth.

THE ROBBER BRIDEGROOM *was first presented on Broadway on October 9, 1976 by John Houseman, Margot Harley, and Michael B. Kapon by arrangement with The Acting Company at the Biltmore Theatre, New York City, with the following cast:*

JAMIE LOCKHART	Barry Bostwick
CLEMMENT MUSGROVE	Stephen Vinovich
ROSAMUND	Rhonda Coullet
SALOME	Barbara Lang
LITTLE HARP	Lawrence John Moss
BIG HARP	Ernie Sabella
GOAT	Trip Plymale
GOAT'S MOTHER	Susan Berger
AIRIE	Jana Schneider
A RAVEN	Carolyn McCurry
KYLE NUNNERY	George Deloy
HARMON HARPER	Gary Epp
NORMAN OGELSBY	B. J. Hardin
QUEENIE BRENNER	Mary Murray
ROSE OTTO	Melinda Tanner
GERRY G. SUMMERS	Dennis Warning
K. K. PONE	Tom Westerman

Book and lyrics by Alfred Uhry
Based on the novella by Eudora Welty
Music composed and arranged by Robert Waldman
Directed by Gerald Freedman
Choreography by Donald Saddler
Scenery by Douglas W. Schmidt
Costumes by Jeanne Button
Lighting by David F. Segal
Associate Producer: Porter Van Zandt
Technical Consultant: Edward Wilchinski, Jr.
Wardrobe Supervisor: Rosalie Lahm
General Managers: McCann & Nugent
Assistant to Director: Matthew Bullock

MUSICAL NUMBERS

"*Once Upon the Natchez Trace*" JAMIE LOCKHART,
ROSAMUND, SALOME,
CLEMMENT MUSGROVE,
LITTLE HARP, BIG
HARP, GOAT, COMPANY

"*Two Heads*" BIG HARP, LITTLE HARP
"*Steal With Style*" JAMIE LOCKHART
"*Rosamund's Dream*" ROSAMUND
"*The Pricklepear Bloom*" SALOME
"*Nothin' Up*" ROSAMUND
"*Deeper in the Woods*" COMPANY
"*Riches*" CLEMMENT MUSGROVE,
JAMIE LOCKHART,
SALOME, ROSAMUND

"*Love Stolen*" JAMIE LOCKHART
"*Poor Tied Up Darlin'*" LITTLE HARP, GOAT
"*Goodbye Salome*" COMPANY
"*Sleepy Man*" ROSAMUND
"*Where Oh Where*" JAMIE LOCKHART,
CLEMMENT MUSGROVE,
ROSAMUND, COMPANY

A musical performed without intermission. The action takes place in and around Rodney, Mississippi.

THE ROBBER BRIDEGROOM

CAST OF CHARACTERS

JAMIE LOCKHART, a gentleman robber
CLEMMENT MUSGROVE, a wealthy planter
SALOME, his second wife
ROSAMUND, his daughter
LITTLE HARP, a robber
BIG HARP, the head of a robber
GOAT, a simpleton
AIRIE, his sister
GOAT'S MOTHER
A RAVEN
RESIDENTS OF RODNEY

The audience enters to an empty set. At curtain time a NARRATOR *enters and speaks to the audience.*

NARRATOR   The town of Rodney, Mississippi isn't very much anymore.
The river moved away and left us high and dry.
Where the landing used to be there's just swamp now.
But we got one hell of a history around here.
The buffaloes were first—beat a path through the woods down to the river.
Then the Natchez Indians—stark naked and holes in their ears the size of peach pits—that's the truth.
They used that buffalo path for a trail and that trail stretched from Nashville all the way down to New Orleans.
They called it the Natchez Trace.
Pretty soon you know what came down the Trace?
A settler.
> (A FIDDLER, *playing, enters from the back of the house and walks toward the stage*)

And another.
> (A SECOND FIDDLER *in another part of the house, also playing, does the same*)

And another.
> (A THIRD MUSICIAN *does the same*)

And another.
> (A FOURTH MUSICIAN *does the same*)

3

And a whole lot more.
> (THE LAST MUSICIAN *does the same. After* ALL *the* MUSICIANS *have entered the* TOWNSPEOPLE *begin to come onstage)*

And the people kept coming.
Men met women.
Couples met preachers.
Neighbors met neighbors.
High life met low life
And everybody just melted together.
> (*The* CALLER *calls the following and the* TOWNSPEOPLE *do a country dance)*

CALLER

All right gentlemen tighten your belt
Ladies breathe in and everybody melt

Men melt this way and ladies melt that
Simmer together like you're cookin' in a vat

Everybody here is everybody's friend
And that's the way the people blend.

Ladies make a chain up and down
And lift your partner—ain't that a load!
And gents to the center and left hand star
And ladies to the center
And a right hand star back the other way
And let's fan out and down and around
And walk the corners back and fore
Allemande left grand right and left
And move right along as grand as you please
And meet your partner on the other side
Honor your corner honor your partner
And everybody rest.

JAMIE   They really had dancin' on the Natchez Trace back in those days, didn't they?

SUE   There was a man named J. W. Loudermilk in Maycomb, Mississippi, and in the year 1795 he went to a dance and he got to dancin' so hard that his body broke off at the bellybutton and the top half went dancin' off to St. Louis and the legs went kickin' off to Tallahassee, and that's the truth.

JAMIE   Remember Jamie Lockhart? They say he could eat half a watermelon, spit out the seeds and recite the Twenty-third Psalm all at the same time. *(General disbelief)* He could! He could.
   (Sings)
   Oh what a man—now this is true
   He had two faces
   So help me God would I lie to you
   One face could scare a person dead
   The other face was so well bred
   Two faces sittin' up there on the same man's head
   I never would stand here and lie in your face
   That's exactly how it happened
   Once upon the Natchez Trace

Jamie Lockhart had a bad face and a good face
   (Sings)
   The good face was like a preacher's prayer
   Completely honest
   So help me God would I lie to you

And the other face was stained with the juice of wild blackberries outta the woods
   (Sings)
   And that face was dark and full of crime

RAVEN (Carolyn McCurry) and JAMIE LOCKHART (Barry Bostwick), the Broadway production.

Looked like he'd steal your bottom dime
And both could talk to a man at the same damn
   time

I never would stand here and lie in your face
That's exactly how it happened
Once upon the Natchez Trace

ROSAMUND   Well what about my great-great-grand-
mother Rosamund?

JAMIE   Yeah, she changed the temperature of the moon!
That's right
   (Sings)
   She was a girl
   Now this is true

ROSAMUND *(Sings)*
   She made the moon hot
   So help me God

JAMIE and ROSAMUND *(Sing)*
   Would we lie to you?

ROSAMUND *(Sings)*
   One night she's sleeping in the raw
   The moon looked down and dropped his jaw
   He roasted hot as the sun from the sight he saw

JAMIE and ROSAMUND *(Sing)*
   We never would stand here and lie in your face
   That's exactly how it happened
   Once upon the Natchez Trace

ALL *(Sing)*
   We never would stand here and lie in your face
   That's exactly how it happened
   Once upon the Natchez Trace

SALOME Talkin' about looks reminds me of the woman called Salome.

JAMIE Yeah, tell 'em that one.

SALOME The story goes that one glance from her caused every bullfrog in Yazoo City to drop dead of heart failure.

JAMIE Honey. She was ugly!

SALOME *(Sings)*
She was a scrawny greedy woman

JAMIE *(Sings)*
Oh what a scrawny greedy woman

SALOME *(Sings)*
She had buzzard eyes
She had crocodile jaws
She had grabby long arms
And her fingers were turkey foot claws
And she lusted after every pair of pants on the
  Natchez Trace!

MUSGROVE And what about her husband, old Clemment Musgrove?

JAMIE Yeah, they say he was the most fortunate man in the Mississippi Territory!

JAMIE and MUSGROVE *(Sing)*
He was a rich and lucky planter

MUSGROVE *(Sings)*
Oh what a rich and lucky planter

He took one little seed
And he stuck it in the ground

And from that little seed
I swear there was cotton all around
And all them cotton plants were 110 feet high
Would I lie?

JAMIE *(Sings)*
Would he lie?

GOAT   Tell us about the famous Goat of Rodney.

JAMIE   Well he wasn't a goat, really. He was a boy.

GOAT   Yeah, but they say he had a brain the size of a scuppernong seed.
(Sings)
Goat was his name

GOAT and JAMIE *(Sing)*
Now this is true

GOAT *(Sings)*
His head was empty
From ear to ear you could see right through

LITTLE HARP   Talkin' about heads reminds me of Little Harp.

JAMIE   I know what you mean. He was the most gruesome robber in the whole history of the Natchez Trace.

GOAT   I thought you was tellin' us about a head.

JAMIE   Let him finish.

LITTLE HARP *(Sings)*
He was a mangey lookin' skunk
When he went by the flowers shrunk

JAMIE *(Sings)*
The willows wept at how he stunk

LITTLE HARP and JAMIE *(Sing)*
He carried everywhere he went his brother's

JAMIE *(Sings)*
Bloody

LITTLE HARP *(Sings)*
Nasty

JAMIE *(Sings)*
Mangey

LITTLE HARP *(Sings)*
Stinky

JAMIE *(Sings)*
Cutoff

JAMIE and LITTLE HARP *(Sing)*
Head in a trunk

JAMIE, LITTLE HARP and BIG HARP *(Sing)*
We never would stand here and lie in your face
That's exactly how it happened
Once upon the Natchez Trace

ALL *(Sing)*
We never would stand here and lie in your face
That's exactly how it happened

JAMIE *(Sings)*
A gent and a robber all in one

ROSAMUND *(Sings)*
A girl who made the moon burn like the sun

SALOME *(Sings)*
> A greedy witch

MUSGROVE *(Sings)*
> A man that rich

GOAT *(Sings)*
> A brain that big

LITTLE HARP *(Sings)*
> A filthy pig

BIG HARP *(Sings)*
> A talkin' head

JAMIE   And like I said a hell of a lot happened around here.

ALL *(Sing)*
> Once upon the Natchez Trace
> Once upon the Natchez Trace

MUSGROVE *(To the* PEOPLE*)*   How are you? I'm Clement Musgrove. I just came up on the boat from New Orleans. Traded my whole tobacco crop for this. *(Holds up moneybag)* But I don't want anybody to see how much gold I got.

A MAN   It's a secret.

JAMIE *(Sings)*
> Now suddenly the day looks sunny
> Yonder comes a planter with a sack of money
> Look that moneybag up and down
> I'll pluck it offa him in Rodney town
> Jamie Lockhart is quick and sharp
> I can always outrob Little Harp

MUSGROVE   I'm afraid some robber's gonna murder me before I get home, and every inn in Rodney has a fearful reputation.

LANDLORD   Oh no! Right this way—how do you do? The Golden Fleece is the place for you.

MUSGROVE   I'm so tired I could sleep standing up. *(Yawning)* How much for a bed?

LANDLORD   For you—ten—sixteen gold pieces!

MUSGROVE   Oh sixteen . . . That's high! I'm a poor man!
   (CROWD *reacts*)

LANDLORD   What? Ain't you Clemment Musgrove, the richest planter in the whole Mississippi Territory?

MUSGROVE   No! *(Then quieter)* I'll take the room. I'll be to myself, won't I? I'm a light sleeper.

LANDLORD   I'm insulted you'd even ask me a thing like that. Of course you will. Unless the Inn fills up. Up the stairs. Second room on the right past the pisspot. The Azalea Room.

MUSGROVE   I don't like the feel of this place.

A CALLER
   Rest the rich man

GIRLS *(As* MUSGROVE *"climbs" up to his room, call)*
   Good night
   Good night
   Up the stairs and turn to the right
   Don't that bed look soft and deep
   Move along—it's time for sleep

Ooooooh! Ahhhhhhhh!
Oooooh! Ahhhhhhhh!
(MUSGROVE *is suspicious*)

LANDLORD Don't worry. You're as safe in this bed as you was in your mama's arms. For the time being. Good night. (HE *goes out of the room, sees* LITTLE HARP) Little Harp!

RAVEN (*To* LITTLE HARP) Turn back, my bonny. Turn away home.

LITTLE HARP I know what I'm doing. Raven, you be a good bird and keep a sharp lookout.

BIG HARP (*In the trunk*) Little Harp! Little Harp!

LITTLE HARP What is it, Big Harp?

BIG HARP Let me outta here! You didn't have to bump me up the stairs so hard and will you quit droppin' me, you little pissant!

LITTLE HARP Quit callin' me names. Damn! You been in a bad mood ever since they cut your head off for stealin' and if you don' stop—

BIG HARP Shut up snivelling. Be thankful you saved my head. Where would you be without it? Now we got to make us a plan before we go in there. No, not the knife, boy. Too messy. What I'd do is yank a board outta the floor and whack that damn planter to kingdom come!

LITTLE HARP I know we fight a lot but I gotta admit you are certainly the brains of this outfit.

BIG HARP Aw. Well, I couldn't operate without you, brother.

BIG HARP and LITTLE HARP *(Sing)*
> Two heads are better than one, brother
> When everything's said and done
> If there's a problem to master
> Two minds can master it faster
> And four eyes are better than two, brother
> For seein' a sticky time through
> Two noses can smell better
> Two throats can yell better
> Two heads are better than one ·
> I can try on my own to get by on my own
> But the fact of the matter remains

BIG HARP and LITTLE HARP *(Sing)*
> What I start every time falls apart every time
> And that's why I'm stickin' to pickin' your brains
> Oh two heads are—

BIG HARP   I think I hear something.

LITTLE HARP   Where? Where? Sorry, brother, I lost my head.

BIG HARP and LITTLE HARP *(Sing)*
> Two heads are better than one, brother
> When everything's said and done

BIG HARP *(Sings)*
> I ponder and mull better

LITTLE HARP *(Sings)*
> I break a skull better

BIG HARP *(Sings)*
> I see the facts better

LITTLE HARP *(Sings)*
> I swing an axe better

BIG HARP *(Sings)*
    I do the plottin'

LITTLE HARP *(Sings)*
    But I do the swattin'

BIG HARP and LITTLE HARP *(Sing)*
    And that's how the business gets done, brother
    Cause two heads are better than one
    Are better than one!
        *(*JAMIE *has entered* MUSGROVE's *room during the song)*

LITTLE HARP   All right, rich planter. Prepare to tangle
with the Harp gang!

JAMIE   Evenin', Little Harp.

LITTLE HARP   What the hell? You're Jamie Lockhart,
aincha? I hear about you all over the territory. Now
what's a fancy swindler like you doin' here?

JAMIE   Believe me, I ain't here through choice. This
spot in this bed happens to be the only place left to
sleep in Rodney tonight. So you just slide on in the
bed like a June breeze. You won't even know I'm
here.

LITTLE HARP   Why don't you get the hell outta here?

JAMIE   Little Harp, I'm tired. Let's make a deal. I won't
do no tricks on you if you don't do no tricks on me.
Thief's honor.

LITTLE HARP   Thief's honor. *(To the trunk)* Don't worry,
brother. I'll just make him *think* I'm sleepin'.

RAVEN   Turn back, my bonny, turn away home.

LITTLE HARP   I'll just put my raven on the headboard for the night.

JAMIE   That bird talks!

LITTLE HARP   Ah-hah.

JAMIE   Bird bites!

LITTLE HARP   Damn! I'm wore out. Good night.

JAMIE   Good night.

LITTLE HARP   Good night.

JAMIE and LITTLE HARP   Good night.

BIG HARP   Good night, little brother.

MUSGROVE *(Sitting bolt upright)*   Good night. Inn fills up fast, don't it. *(JAMIE puts a knife to MUSGROVE's throat)* Sweet Jesus, you gonna kill me?

JAMIE   No, he is. Come get in the closet.

MUSGROVE   What's that?

JAMIE   Sugar cane. Want a piece?

MUSGROVE   No thank you.
        (THEY hide. RAVEN wakes LITTLE HARP up)

LITTLE HARP   I musta' dozed off. Good, they're asleep. Here I go, big brother. Piece of pine this is Little Harp got you by the tail. Now go to work and ruin these two sleepin' fools. *(Whacking at bed)* Good! Good again! One more time! There ain't one whole bone left between 'em. Done, Big Harp.

BIG HARP   Good work, brother.

LITTLE HARP   Good night.
> (HE *falls asleep.* JAMIE *and* MUSGROVE *come out of the closet*)

JAMIE   Good mornin'.

LITTLE HARP   Good mornin'.

MUSGROVE   Good mornin'.

LITTLE HARP   Good mornin'. Holy Mother, bogeys for sure!
> (HE *dives out of the window, leaving behind the trunk and the* RAVEN)

MUSGROVE   Why, you saved my life! Thank you, Mr.—Mr.—

JAMIE   Lockhart. Jamie Lockhart.

MUSGROVE   I'd like to give you something, Mr. Lockhart.

JAMIE   Jamie. I'll just take his talking bird if you don't mind.

MUSGROVE   Take something of mine, Jamie.

JAMIE   No thank you, Mr. Musgrove.

MUSGROVE   Clemment.

JAMIE   That's probably all the money you got in this world, Clemment.

MUSGROVE   Oh no! I got a big plantation.

JAMIE   Big plantation?

MUSGROVE Yeah, I got cotton fields and indigo fields and a house with twenty-two Corinthian columns. But I got an even greater treasure.

JAMIE Greater treasure?

MUSGROVE My daughter—Rosamund. She's so beautiful she keeps the memory of my wife alive and ever green in my heart.

JAMIE Oh, your wife's dead? I'm sorry. Just you and your daughter live on that big plantation?

MUSGROVE No. There's my second wife, Salome. She ain't as beautiful as my first wife but she's a woman to reckon with. She's deviled me to get as rich as I am and even now she ain't satisfied. Jamie, will you come for dinner on Sunday and meet my girl?

JAMIE That's awfully kind of you but I think I will. And Clemment, don't ride out of town on the Trace. It's crawlin' with robbers. I don't want any of them to lay hands on you now. Take the cutoff path and you'll be all right.

MUSGROVE Bless you, Jamie. You want to keep me safe, don't you?

JAMIE Till Sunday.

MUSGROVE Till Sunday.

JAMIE *(Tossing moneybag)* Clemment.

MUSGROVE That boy don't have a dishonest bone in his body.
     (Exits)

JAMIE *(Sings)*

I guess you wonder why
I let this rich man by
And passed up all his money with a smile
A sitting duck you say
I let him get away
Well the answer is I steal with style

I don't come up and rob
Like some dumb country slob
I let my treasure dangle for a while
I let that treasure lay
And flatter it away
Yes the answer is I steal with style

With my dark face on I am the Bandit of the
    Woods
When I'm him it's easier to snatch the stolen goods
But with Jamie Lockhart the stealin' ain't the same
It's a finagling, angling game

So I let that rich man go

Because I truly know
This place of his must be a treasure pile

I'll ride out to his house

And play some cat and mouse
And I promise you
I'll steal with style

On the evenin' I was born the stars were lookin'
    fine
It was written in them stars that I was gonna shine
I was born for faking and taking come what may
In my finaglin' anglin' way
Yes I guess it's just my fate

To always be first rate
To outfox all them others by a mile
I'll hit that rich man's farm
And ladle out my charm
And I promise you
Oh yes I promise you
I guarantee to you
I'll steal with style

THE RAVEN   Turn back my bonny, turn away home!
    (JAMIE leaves with RAVEN)

BIG HARP *(In the trunk)*   Help, goddamit, help!

LITTLE HARP *(Struggling in)*   I'm comin'. I'm comin', Big
Harp. *(Looks around)* I'll be damned. The ghost of
Jamie Lockhart stole our raven! That ghost is gonna
pay for this!
    (HE pushes the trunk off)

SALOME   Bring home the husband!
    (Sings)
  Gallop thru the live oak
  Gallop thru the pine
  Gallop thru the moss to wifey thine
  Gallop thru the sweetshrub
  Queen Anne's lace
  Soon you'll spy my fair dear face
  Gallop thru the dogwood
  Columbine
  All of nature's blessin's are mine
  Beauty brains taste talent wit warmth
  Gallop to your treasure
  Thy wife
Rosamund! Rosamund!

ROSAMUND (Patti LuPone), NEIGHBOR (Brooks Baldwin),
LITTLE HARP (J. W. Harper), and SALOME (Mary Lou
Rosato), The Acting Company.
Photo by Robert M. Lightfoot III.

ROSAMUND *(Singing dreamily to herself)*
    A fine young king on a stallion tall
    Will to my window ride
    His eyes will sing and his heart will call
    For me to be his bride
    Rosamund
    Rosamund he will say

SALOME Rosamund!

ROSAMUND *(Sings)*
    Rosamund
    Rosamund
    Rosamund
    Come away

SALOME Rosamund!

ROSAMUND *(Sings)*
    Then a finer king on a finer horse
    Will come the self-same day
    And he will bring his crown of course
    To tempt my love away
    Rosamund
    Rosamund
    He will say

SALOME Rosamund!

ROSAMUND *(Sings)*
    Rosamund! Rosamund! Rosamund.
    Come away

SALOME Rosamund—

ROSAMUND *(Goes to* SALOME. *Sweetly)* Were you callin me, stepmother?

SALOME Well, lazy thang, git out and fetch me fresh herbs fer the pot.

ROSAMUND I went yestiddy.

SALOME And yer goin' today. Fresh herbs from the indigo field. Git.

ROSAMUND Oh, all right.

SALOME An' if you cum back without a apron full of herbs I'll slap you knock-kneed. Bye!
    (ROSAMUND exits)
    (To the COMPANY)
There's panthers in the indigo field. Maybe today's my lucky day!

MUSGROVE *(Entering)* Hay, wife.

SALOME Hello, honey.

MUSGROVE Well, the place looks fine! I bin missing it the whole two weeks of my journey!

SALOME The place! What about me?

MUSGROVE Wait 'til I tell ya whut happened to me. I was over ta . . .

SALOME Look! My fingernails grew a inch while you wuz gone.

MUSGROVE Well look at that!

SALOME Ain't a woman from here to Biloxi kin grow cartiledge as fast as I kin. It's a known fact.

MUSGROVE Salome, like I wuz tellin ya, I wuz over ta th' inn at Rodney. . . . Guess who cum inta th' room with me, he got inta th' bed with me. Little Harp! He tried ta steal my moneybag, but . . .

SALOME   He didn't git it did he??

MUSGROVE   No, see, because this other fella—Jamie Lockhart—

SALOME   How did the tradin' go with the King's men? I suppose you got taken again.

MUSGROVE   Oh no! It went fine—excellent!

SALOME   Well, where is it?

MUSGROVE   *(Holding moneybag)*   Looka here!

SALOME   Fine? Excellent? For all that tobacco you got this? If I'd a traded that tobacco we'd a got whut it was worth. *(To the* PEOPLE*)* It ain't my fault we ain't rich.

MUSGROVE   We are rich.

SALOME   I mean rich, Clemment. Feel my forehead.

MUSGROVE   Have you got a fever?

SALOME   That's my brain workin'. *(To the* PEOPLE*)* Where are the presents you brung?

MUSGROVE   Right here. Wait'll you see whut I brung ya. Here's a soup ladle—and sum sewin needles— and a feather duster—and sum muscadine wine like you love.

SALOME   I'm gonna need that wine!

MUSGROVE   And that's not all! Whut do you think of

this green silk dress—and this petticoat stitched with gold?

SALOME   Clemment! You never brought nuthin' lak this before! Ain't they elegant. Oh, thank you!

MUSGROVE   They're fer Rosamund.

SALOME   Fer Rosamund?

MUSGROVE   Like you said I got ta quit babyin' her. And this is the growd up dress that'll do it. Where is she?

SALOME   Out in the indigo field gatherin' herbs.

MUSGROVE   You sint her out inta th' woods. There's bandits in them woods . . . I told you Little Harp's bin hangin' roun' here . . . And there's wil' animals.

SALOME   Oh! Rosamund's a big girl. Lak you sed you got ta quit babyin' her . . .

ROSAMUND *(Coming in)*   Hey, Daddy!

MUSGROVE   Rosamund! Let me look at you. Oh, you look fine, baby. Look whut I brung you.

ROSAMUND   That's fer me? Daddy, thank you!

SALOME   Where's them herbs?

ROSAMUND   I had 'em. I had a whole apronful comin' home thru the woods when this, uh, panther come at me from behind a holly bush.

SALOME   A panther!

ROSAMUND   Yes. He was blue. A rich midnight blue. And he musta been eleven feet long.

MUSGROVE   Baby, is this true?

ROSAMUND   Of course, Daddy.

SALOME   Of course, Daddy. She's the biggest liar on the Natchez Trace.

ROSAMUND   And then he blinked his eyes and picked me up by the sash and carried me home and shook me out on the front doorstep. Course all the herbs fell outta my apron when he did that.

MUSGROVE   Angel, you got ta quit lyin' so much.

SALOME   She gits away with murder! Git back out in that field an' gather me my herbs.

ROSAMUND   Daddy, kin I try on my new dress?

SALOME   My herbs!

MUSGROVE   Try it on, baby! I bin lookin' fer that sight all the way up from New Orleans.

SALOME   I thank we oughta put it away until she's a little bit older, Clemment.
     (ROSAMUND *leaves*)

MUSGROVE   You know, she's lookin' more lak her mother every day. (HE *leaves*) I'll tell you.

SALOME   He's always bringing up that beautiful first wife of his. Ain't he got eyes?
     (*Sings*)
     I bear a bitter truth
     My bosom droops with gloom
     The world prefers the lilybud
     To the pricklepear bloom
     Oh Daddy—can I try on my dress—oh baby, of

course, I've been looking for that sight all the way
from New Orleans.

(Sings)
Tragedy of my youth
While seekin' out my groom
The world preferred the lilybud
To the pricklepear bloom

Fair pricklepear
Seldom seen
Rare radiant spikey queen
Thy glorious name is mud
For the world prefers the lilybud
Look what I brought you, Salome—a soup ladle,
some sewing needles and a feather duster.

(Sings)
I wear my finest dress
And glide across the room
But men prefer the lilybud
To the pricklepear bloom

She wears some tacky mess
And mopes around like doom
And they still prefer the lilybud
To the pricklepear bloom

Fair pricklepear
Flower gem
Rare beauty from smell to stem
Thy pleasure would come up rich
If it wasn't for that lilybitch
Maybe them panthers won't get her—but somethin'
will.

(Sings)
That's why I get no rest

I conjure day and night
I dream of somethin' glorious
Like a lilybud blight

When lilybud is pressed
Into the book of doom
They'll fall on their faces to pick
The pricklepear bloom
  (After song)
I'm gonna git rid of Miss Prissypants fer good!
  (SALOME *goes among the* COMPANY. GOAT *is the caller)*

GOAT *(Sings)*
  Grab yore mate and skedaddle all
  Ole Salome's eye may fall on you
    (SHE *searches among the* COMPANY. THEY *fly out of her way)*
  Swing to yore neighbor—don't dare pause
  Buzzard woman may sink her claws in you!
    (Quick pace as EVERYBODY *dodges* SALOME*)*
  Seek for a nook to hide behind

  Hmmm hmmm hmmm hmmm
  Looks as if she's set her mind

SALOME *(Sugary voice)*   Hay there, boy.

GOAT *(Sings)*
  On me!
  Aggggggh!
    *(*TOWNSPEOPLE *remain where* THEY *are)*

SALOME   My what a fine looking boy!

GOAT *(Bellowing)*   Maaaaaa! Maaaaaa!

SALOME   You're the one named Goat, aincha?

GOAT   Maaaaa!
*(*GOAT'S MOTHER *emerges from the* COMPANY, *a granite-faced, pursed-mouth creature)*

GOAT'S MOTHER *(As* SHE *comes)*   What is it, stupid? Quit hollerin' or I'll change the shape of your head with a skillet. *(Sees* RICH LADY, *changes tone)* Yess ma'am?

SALOME   This yore son?

GOAT'S MOTHER   My onliest. Ain' I lucky? I got jis' him and his sister Airie looks jis' like him.

SALOME   I bet you wish you had eight like him.

GOAT'S MOTHER   Eight like Goat? One? Two? Three? Four? Five? Six? Seven? Eight?
(Music starts)

SALOME   A fine looking boy.

GOAT'S MOTHER   Yes ma'am.

SALOME   I bet you raised him right.

GOAT'S MOTHER   Oh yes ma'am.

SALOME   I bet he minds.

GOAT'S MOTHER *(Sensing something)*   Oh yessum. He surely does.

SALOME   Un hunh. I bet he does whatever you tell him. Never no questions.

GOAT'S MOTHER   Never. No questions.

SALOME   Well, Goat, how'd you like to work for me?

GOAT   No.

GOAT'S MOTHER *(Giving him a whack)*   He'll be proud to.

GOAT   What's the pay?

SALOME   These peaches I personally pickled right now and a *suckling pig* when the job is done.

GOAT'S MOTHER   Agreed. Goodbye.
> (SHE *snatches the peaches and leaves.* SALOME *and* GOAT *lead the* DANCERS)

SALOME *(As* THEY *dance)*   My little stepdaughter.

TOWNSPEOPLE   My little stepdaughter.

SALOME   Out in the indigo field.

TOWNSPEOPLE   Out in the indigo field.

SALOME   Pickin' herbs.

TOWNSPEOPLE   Pickin' herbs.

SALOME   Right at the lip of the ravine.

TOWNSPEOPLE   Right at the lip of the ravine.
> (SHE *pantomimes a push which the* TOWNSPEOPLE *repeat)*

SALOME   Bring me a piece of her dress.

TOWNSPEOPLE   Bring me a piece of her dress.

SALOME   For proof.

TOWNSPEOPLE   For proof.

SALOME   And you got you a suckling pig.

TOWNSPEOPLE   And you got you a suckling pig.

GOAT You ain't spoke on a deaf ear. Said is done.

SALOME Rosamund! Rosamund! Guess what! I'm fixin'
to make my famous cracker pie.

ROSAMUND *(Making a face)* Ooooooo.

SALOME Get me some herbs.

ROSAMUND Stepmother, all the herbs from here to
Jerusalem ain't gonna help yore cracker pie.

SALOME Get 'em. And get the fresh ones on the far
side of the indigo field. Right near the lip of the
ravine.

ROSAMUND Lemme change my dress.

SALOME No time fer that.

ROSAMUND Stepmother! I'll ruin it!

SALOME That's because you're fool enough to wear it.
Now git. And if you come back without an apron full
of them herbs you'll find your butt up between your
shoulderblades. Bye.
    (ROSAMUND goes off. SALOME spurs GOAT into action.
    HE follows)

ROSAMUND All day!
    (Throughout the following song GOAT is at intervals
    trying to carry out his mission. HE sneaks carefully up
    behind ROSAMUND, but SHE always turns around at
    the last minute, sending GOAT scurrying back silently
    to hide somewhere. SHE is never aware of GOAT's
    presence)
    (Sings)
  There's nothin' up

Another damn day of nothing up
I'm tight in my skin
And hot in my clothes
And Lord God knows it's cause there's nothing up
Come on come on now
Stop! My birdbrain dreaming gets nothing up

Ain't nothing up
My regular run of nothing up
Mesquitas to slap
And chiggers to swat
How come I got me so much nothin' up
Come on come on now
No! I'll never wish me no nothing up

But boy
I'd love to turn around and see a boy
But whoa
Of course there really isn't one I know
So I'll dream him up
Yes he's there
Handsome dog
Sexy hair
Stealing up
Gaining ground
Coming close
Not a sound
I hear his breath
I sense his hands
He's near so near
And here he stands
Oh boy
But when I turn around of course there never ain't
   no boy

No boy
No boy
No boy

Oh boy boy boy boy boy
There's nothing up
Ain't anything here but nothing up
I lean on a tree
And lay on the grass
And time don't pass 'cause there ain't nothin' up
Come on come on come on please
Someone come from somewhere
Start something up.
Ain't nothin' up—shit
(GOAT *has scurried to hide.* ROSAMUND *finishes her song in disgust. Suddenly* JAMIE *enters, startling them both.* JAMIE *is now dressed in his robber disguise*)

JAMIE *(Pleasant)*   Mornin'.

ROSAMUND   Whut do you want, robber?

JAMIE   'At's a mighty fine dress yore wearin' out fer nothin'.

ROSAMUND   All my dresses are like this. This un's the worst I got. I don't care whut happens to it.

JAMIE   Good. 'Cause I'm takin' it along with me.

ROSAMUND   Whut? Who tole you to do that?

JAMIE   Nobody tole me and nobody needs to tell me nothin'. I think of everythin' for myself. I'm the Bandit of the Woods. Gimme that dress before you git sliced up.

ROSAMUND   Why do you want my dress?

JAMIE   It's a treasure. Hurry up.

ROSAMUND   Are you sure you're the Bandit of the Woods? *(JAMIE gets a knife out)* You kin have my dress then. But not one other thang.

JAMIE   Well, what's that?

ROSAMUND   My petticoat.

JAMIE   Looks to be stitched with gold.

ROSAMUND   All a mine are.

JAMIE   Hand it over!

ROSAMUND   I never heard of a robber stealin' ladies' underwear.

JAMIE   There's always a first time. Gimme them things.
      (SHE hands him the petticoat)

ROSAMUND   Was you born of a woman? For the sake of your pore mother leave me my drawers. Imagine if sumbody'd cum and done this to her.

JAMIE   She'da loved it. Now gimme them thangs.

ROSAMUND   You better know my Daddy kills an average of seventeen bandits a year. And I got eleven brothers and the shortest one is a head taller than you are. You kin jist bet they'll git you for this and hang you to a tree before you're a hour away.

JAMIE   Then hurry. I better git goin' if a father and eleven sons are about to be after me. But doan worry. I kin take all twelve as they come. *(SHE gives him the rest of her clothes and covers herself by letting down her hair)* Yer hair's a lucky length.

ROSAMUND You fixin' to steal that too?

JAMIE I don't thank so. But I will take them golden
hairpins, thank ya.

ROSAMUND Whut else you takin'?

JAMIE Thass all. My work is done. I'm tired. I'm goin'
home. No. Wait. Would you ruther I kill you an' save
yore name or will you go home nekkid?

ROSAMUND Kill me! Heavens, no. Life is sweet. I'll go
home naked.

JAMIE Okay. Have it your way. *(Gathers up his clothes
and hollers as* HE *leaves)* Success!
(Exits)

A CALLER Let's search out the daughter.
            *(*DANCERS *form groups.* SALOME *and* MUSGROVE
            enter and call from opposite parts of the stage)

TOWNSPEOPLE *(Calling as* DANCERS *move, sing)*
    Where oh where's my baby darlin'
    Where oh where's my baby darlin'
    Where oh where's my baby darlin'
    She's been gone a long time.
        *(*TOWNSPEOPLE *call "Rosamund" eight times)*

TOWNSPEOPLE *(Sing)*
    Maybe she tripped and fell down the holler
    Maybe she tripped and fell down the holler
    Maybe she tripped and fell down the holler
    We should git some word soon
        *(*TOWNSPEOPLE *call "Rosamund" eight times)*

TOWNSPEOPLE *(Sing)*
    Let's hire men and go out searchin'

ROSAMUND (Patti LuPone) and COMPANY, The Acting Company.
Photo by Robert M. Lightfoot III.

Let's hire men and go out searchin'
Let's hire men and go out searchin'
Hope she hadn't bin hurt none
    (TOWNSPEOPLE *call "Rosamund" eight times*)

TOWNSPEOPLE *(Sing)*
    Let's gather wood and make a coffin
    Gather wood and make a coffin
    Gather wood and make a coffin
    Jist in case we need one
    Poor little baby darlin'!
        (SALOME *and* MUSGROVE *are in their house*)

SALOME *(In a fine mood)*   My! Ain't the skunk cabbage
beautiful this year?

MUSGROVE   How cum yer only settin' two places for
supper?

SALOME   Well, honey, I thank maybe we got ta prepare
for sum terrible news. (ROSAMUND *enters, naked*) All
right, missy, where's them herbs?

MUSGROVE   Rosamund! Gettin' to look more like her
mother . . . The child's nekkid as a jaybird! *(Covers
her with his coat)* What happened to you, baby?

SALOME   I don't believe it!

MUSGROVE   She ain't even said nothing yet. Now tell
the truth, Rosamund.

ROSAMUND   I'se in the indigo field pickin' herbs fer the
pot and I'se sangin' this little song.
    (Sings)
    Ain't nothin' up
    Another damn day of nothin' up

I'm tight in my skin
And—hot

MUSGROVE   Quiet! What happened whin you finished
singin'?

ROSAMUND   Well. Suddenly there come this big, tall
bandit with berrystains on his face. Said he's the
Bandit of the Woods. He said that's a fine dress
you're wearin' out fer nothin'—Oh, Daddy, it was
my New Orleans dress and he took it and my petticoat stitched with gold an' my golden hair pins an'
everything.

MUSGROVE   Sweet Jesus! What next?

ROSAMUND   He run off.

MUSGROVE   He run off?

ROSAMUND   Yes, Daddy. I swear.

SALOME   Thass right. A panther brung her home by
the sash yestiddy and today the Bandit o' the Woods
stole her nekkid and run off. Liar!

MUSGROVE   Baby, maybe you fell in the Bayou and
ruined yer dress. We won' punish ya.

ROSAMUND   Unh unh. It's the truth!

SALOME   We'll see about that. You jes sit right there,
and tell us what happined over and over and over. If
you vary wun tee-niney detail in the tellin' I'll nail
you for the harlot you are.

ROSAMUND   Okay. I'se out in the indigo field pickin'
herbs for the pot singin' this little song—
    (Sings)

Ain't nothin' up
Another damn day of nothin' up
I'm tight in my skin
And hot—

MUSGROVE   Quiet! Honey, just leave out the song.

ROSAMUND *(Telling a story)*   This big tall bandit come up and he said 'Mornin'' and I said 'What do you want, robber?' He said, 'At's a might fine dress you're wearin' out fer nothin'.' *(The lights dim as time passes)* I said, 'All my dresses are like this. This un's the worst I got. I don't care what happens to it.' He said 'Good cause I'm takin' it along with me.' I said 'Whut who tole you to . . .'

SALOME   That's the thirty-second time! It must be the truth.

MUSGROVE   Where did the bastard go? I'll strang him to a tree fer this!

ROSAMUND   Yes! I tole him you would!

MUSGROVE   You did? Oh. Wait. I got a better idea! It jist so happens that the most daring man in the whole Mississippi Territory is comin' here for dinner to-morra afternoon.

A MAN   Who's that?

MUSGROVE   Jamie Lockhart kin catch this fiend and avenge pore Rosamund's honor.

GOAT *(Crashing in)*   I'm back . . . Good evenin' to ya!

SALOME   Well, who is this? Mus' be sum beggar boy. I'll care for him outside. *(Leads him away as* MUS-

GROVE *carries* ROSAMUND *off*) Yes, my son. How kin I help you? (SHE *hauls him out of earshot*) Well? Did you folla her?

GOAT Lak the lamb to school. I wint out to the indigo field and whin she got ta the very edge of the ravine—

SALOME Yes?

GOAT I'se about ta give her a good push like you said whin this robber come and stole her clothes.

SALOME *(Anxiously interrupting)* Is she de-flowered?

GOAT De what?
(SHE *clouts him.* HE *hollers*)

MUSGROVE Salome, you all right out there?

SALOME Yes, sugar. This pore child has hurt hisself. I'm tendin' to it. You ain't got the sense God give a lemon. Whut happened when she wuz nekkid?

GOAT I shut my eyes for that. My mama tole me—

GOAT'S MOTHER *(As* GOAT *mouths the words)* Don't never look on no nekkid girl.

SALOME How come you didn't do the deed when she wuz comin' home?

GOAT You said brang a piece of the dress and I'd get a suckling pig so I din' folla the girl. I follad the dress.

SALOME Where's the dress then?

GOAT That robber feller took it away with him on his horse.

SALOME   Then what wuz you doing all day?

GOAT   Lookin' for horse turds.

SALOME   Idiot. From now on I want you to folla Rosamund evawhere she goes. All right?

GOAT   First I would like my pay.

SALOME   Here! Take it then!
(Boxes his ears hard)

GOAT   That's enough. I didn' work that hard.
(HE *runs off*)

SALOME   I better do it myself. Rosamund! Rosamund! Sweetheart! *(Gathers a hatchet up and goes to* ROSAMUND'*s bed. A lump in the bed.* SALOME *looks in dismay)* Oh my God! She ain' here! Whar did she go?
(SALOME *exits.* COMPANY *appears.* ROSAMUND *enters, as if waiting for something.* JAMIE *appears from somewhere else)*

THE COMPANY *(Swaying as* THEY *sing)*
    Comes a boy
    He walks so steady
    Comes a girl
    She feels so ready for a stroll
    Deeper in the woods
        (JAMIE *and* ROSAMUND *walk in the woods)*

JAMIE   I thought all yer dresses wuz so fine.

ROSAMUND   This 'un belongs to my maid. I'se afraid I'd meet you again.

JAMIE   Thin why'd ya come?

COMPANY *(Sings)*
>How her eyes they do the pleadin'
>And his arm it does the leadin'
>To their goal
>Deeper in the woods
>Ah the music of swollen streams
>And the rushing of waterfalls
>How the mystery calls them deeper in the woods

ROSAMUND Where we goin'?

JAMIE We? You comin' with me?

COMPANY *(Sings)*
>Up the hills and down the hollows
>How he strides and how she follows
>As they stray deeper in the woods

ROSAMUND What's the matter? You outta breath?

JAMIE I got plenny of breath.

ROSAMUND Thin whut're you puffin' fer?

COMPANY *(Sings)*
>And they come across a clearing
>Past the sound of human hearing
>Where they lay deeper in the woods
>Ah the whisper of open caves
>And the tremble of mighty pines
>How the spell of it twines them
>Deeper in the woods

>Ah the music of swollen streams
>And the rushing of waterfalls
>How the mystery calls them deeper in the woods
>Comes a boy—he walks so steady

Comes a girl—she feels so ready
(The TOWNSPEOPLE *have slowly closed in on* JAMIE *and* ROSAMUND *so that we can't see them anymore)*

A MAN *(To the audience)* And he stopped and laid her on the ground and there he robbed her of that which he had left her the day before.
(SALOME *approaches)*

SALOME Flushed, aincha, fer this hour a the mornin'? I saw you sneakin' home at sunup. Have you forgot, Mr. Jamie Lockhart's comin' to save yer honor today? Though I must say it looks a little late in the game fer that.

ROSAMUND Jamie Lockhart? Comin' to save me from the bandit?

SALOME That's right and the house has to be spotless. Yore Daddy says everythang has got to look perfick fer Jamie Lockhart or he woan want to avenge yer honor with that fiend.

ROSAMUND Whut if Jamie Lockhart doan like the way I look?

SALOME Well, stupid thang, I reckon he woan go after the bandit.

ROSAMUND *(An idea forming)* Stepmother, lissen. I'll take care of everythang. Why doan you go take you a nice long beauty bath.

SALOME That's whut I'm fixin' ta do an if everythang ain't glorious fer Mr. Lockhart I'll kick yore ass ta Memphis.
(Exits)

ROSAMUND *(To the* COMPANY*)* I got s' much ta do I might jist work myself ragged. I might git to look so ragged maybe Mr. Lockhart won't want ta save me even.

> *(*COMPANY *forms working groups.* ROSAMUND *dashes among the groups, doing most of the work)*

ENSEMBLE *(Sings)*
> Company's comin'
> Company's comin'
> Company's comin'
> Sweep the floor
> Soap the floor
> Scrub the floor
>
> Company's comin'
> Shine the floor to make a good impression
>
> Company's comin'
> Find the hen
> Kill the hen
> Pluck the hen
>
> Company's comin'
> Bake the hen to make a good impression
>
> Company's comin'
> Pick the greens
> Sort the greens
> Clean the greens
>
> Company's comin'
> Boil the greens to make a good impression
>
> Company's comin'
> Make the candles
> Shine the holders

Beat the biscuits
Iron the curtains
Pump the water
Wipe the windows
Plump the pillows
Light the fire
Sweep the ashes
To make a good impression
Company's comin'
Company's comin'
Git the chairs
Wipe the rungs
Shine the seats
Scrub the bowls
Pass the plates
Lick the spoons
Find a vase
Pick some buds
Make it nice
To make a good impression
(ROSAMUND *collapses under the table, exhausted from the work.* SHE *is a disheveled mess)*

MUSGROVE   This is my home, Jamie.

JAMIE   Twenty-two Corinthian columns just as you described them. And these steps!

MUSGROVE   Marble! But just wait until you get a look at Rosamund.

JAMIE   No treasure, even the palace you have here, can outshine the charms of a magnificent woman.
(SALOME *enters, dressed in her version of finery)*

SALOME   Como esta!

MUSGROVE This is my wife, Salome, and this here's Jamie Lockhart.

SALOME Well, Jamie Lockhart! Jamie Lockhart! Clemment has spoken of nothing else since he got home. He never told me you wuz, so, uh, young.

JAMIE And he never told me you were so, uh, remarkable. Why, that's—

SALOME Gold.

JAMIE Sewed right into your dress! Lovely! Where's my manners? I brought you this nothin' of a gift.

SALOME A brooch! Well, I'm jist all fiddle fingers this evening. Would you pin it on fer me, Mr. Lockhart?

JAMIE Always glad to oblige a lovely lady. Look at them silver dishes! Where would you like it?

SALOME Careful, I'm tinder in there!

MUSGROVE Where's Rosamund?

SALOME I ain't seen her all day! I had to tidy this whole house by myself.

JAMIE And it looks fine. That's French inlaid furniture, ain't it?

SALOME Why thank you fer noticin', Mr. Lockhart. You appreciate beauty when you see it, don't ya?

MUSGROVE Rosamund! What's the matter? Jamie gimme a hand here! This here's Jamie Lockhart!

ROSAMUND Pleased to meet you.

JAMIE I brung you this nuthin' of a—

(ROSAMUND *takes the gift without a word. Her hair is hanging in her face and* SHE *is dirty.* SHE *and* JAMIE *do not recognize each other, as* HE *doesn't have on his berrystain*)

MUSGROVE Look a there. Gold hairpins. Now that is nice, Rosamund. Where's yore tongue, daughter? I never seen her this way. Somethin' musta scrambled her brains. Ain't she pritty, tho', Jamie? Rosamund, pull yourself together!

SALOME And while she's doin' that, I'll take Mr. Lockhart for a stroll in my thornbush garden.

MUSGROVE Rosamund! Whut is it, baby? Jamie, you kin see whut her experience with this menace ta womankind has done? You got ta avenge her honor. There's a great reward in it fer you.

JAMIE Whut is this reward, Mr. Musgrove?

MUSGROVE Don't wear the bowl, honey. Avenge my daughter and she is yours!

JAMIE Marriage?

SALOME Marriage?

MUSGROVE Marriage?
      (Sings)
   Marriage is riches
   It's batches of riches
   It's patches on britches so lovingly sewn
   It's settin' on porches
   And bitin' on peaches
   And watchin' the moon rise
   Together alone

Riches
Riches
Marriage is riches
Riches

JAMIE *(Sings)*
Yes
How much land do you own?

MUSGROVE *(Sings)*
'Bout ten thousand acres
But we're talkin' about marriage
And marriage is riches
Sich as I've shown

JAMIE *(Sings)*
Marriage is riches
Sich as you've shown

SALOME *(Sings)*
Marriage is lovin'
It's hours of blisses
And powerful kisses
I shouldn't say where
It's womanly shudders
On muscular shoulders
And rumpled up linens
All tangled with hair
Riches
Riches
Lovin' is riches
Riches

JAMIE *(Sings)*
Yes
Whut's that thang on yore head?

SALOME *(Sings)*
    A diamon' tiarry
    But we're talking about loving

MUSGROVE *(Sings)*
    No, we're talking about marriage

SALOME *(Sings)*
    Yes, we're talkin' about marriage
    And marriage is riches
    Sich as I said

JAMIE *(Sings)*
    Marriage is riches
    Sich as you said

MUSGROVE *(Sings)*
    Settle down son
    Take a wife and git homey
    Just lak me and Salome
    Salome!

SALOME *(Sings)*
    I wus jist bein homey

JAMIE *(Sings)*
    Excuse me
    You wuz startin' to show me
    That marriage is riches
    Which reminds me
    Ain't this candlestick golden

SALOME *(Sings)*
    And my bed is brocaded
    Cum and see how I made it

JAMIE *(Sings)*
> No I got to be going

SALOME *(Sings)*
> But you couldn't be goin'
> We wuz talkin' about bedspreads

JAMIE *(Sings)*
> We wuz talkin' about riches

MUSGROVE *(Sings)*
> We wuz talkin' about marriage

ROSAMUND *(Sings)*
> And here I am all ragged and dirty
> If you doan come kiss me
> I'll run like a turkey

MUSGROVE *(Sings)*
> Yes marriage is riches

ROSAMUND *(Sings)*
> I'd luv ta be wed
> Luv ta be wed

MUSGROVE Rosamund!

ROSAMUND Jamie!

JAMIE Miz Musgrove!

ALL *(Sing)*
> Marriage is riches, sich as we said!

MUSGROVE Well, son, what do you say?

JAMIE Lemme ponder on it, Clemment. Your daughter

certainly is—something, but I ain't a man to marry lightly. What if I let you know by Winsday?

MUSGROVE   Winsday, then, but no later. There's a pack of fellas after Rosamund's hand.

JAMIE   Well, I'm warning you, Clemment. I just might steal your treasure right out from under you!

MUSGROVE   Son, that would be wonderful.

JAMIE   Miz Musgrove, Miss Rosamund, Clemment, I can't leave without saying that you are living in the house with the two most amazing females I ever saw in my life.

MUSGROVE   See ya Winsday.

JAMIE   Winsday.
   (HE *exits*)

MUSGROVE   Isn't that Jamie a fine lookin' fella?

SALOME   Is he? I didn't notice. (*To* ROSAMUND) All right, missy. That's enough play actin'. Doan you think for one second that I don' know whu's goin on in yore head. Now git out in the kitchen and start—

MUSGROVE   I'll help you in the kitchen, Salome. Let my baby rest. (SALOME *and* MUSGROVE *exit*) I think the dinner was a total success.

JAMIE   This Musgrove girl is even worse than I figured. Makes me ache all the more fer that girl I met in the woods. I cain't git my mind off the way she looked with that yella hair fallin over them shoulders!

ROSAMUND   (*To the* COMPANY) Jamie Lockhart prisses

around lak a pea hen. I'll never let him save me. I got to find where my robber lives.

JAMIE *(Calling)*
> Little piece of sugar cane
> Where are you
> Seek me out whutever you do
> Look to the left—look to the right
> Steal away into the night
> The owl screams—the woods are black
> Little piece of sugar cane don't turn back
>
> If somethin' hollers from a tree
> Don't be skeered just think of me
> The nightbugs fly against your cheek
> Walk the rocks along the creek
> > (ROSAMUND *makes her way to his house while* HE *calls)*
>
> Your shoe gits wet your hem gits torn
> But you know my need 'n' I know yorn
> Little piece of sugar cane
> Push ahead
> Love will lead you to my bed
> Come on
> Come on
> My little piece of sugar cane
> Come on
> Come on
> That's right.

THE RAVEN *(Sings)*
> With my dark face on I am the Bandit of the Woo . . .
> *(Spoken)*

Turn back, my bonny. Turn away home.
> (GOAT *hears this and leaves quick.* ROSAMUND *never knows* HE's *there*)

ROSAMUND   Oh shet up. You stupid bird, you thank I'm lissenin' to you after I come all this damn way? *(Calls into house)* Hay!

GOAT   Hay!

ROSAMUND   Hay in there!

GOAT   Hay in there!

ROSAMUND *(Goes in—sees mess)*   I wonder whut I'm gittin' myself inta. My New Orleans dress! I found my robber! This place is a mess.

ENSEMBLE *(Sings)*
> Yer lover's comin'
> Sweep the floor
> Bake the bread
> Hide the trash
> Yer lover's comin'
>> (ROSAMUND *exits*)
> Yer lover's comin'
> Sweep the floor
> Bake the bread
> Hide the trash
> Yer lover's comin'
> Make it nice to make a good impression
> Yer lover's comin'
> Change yer dress
> Comb yer hair
> Pinch yer cheeks
> Yer lover's comin'

Make the bed to make a good impression
> (ROSAMUND *enters in her stolen dress.* JAMIE *enters*)

JAMIE   Whut're you doin' here?

ROSAMUND   My cornbread's burning! *(Races to oven)* It's okay. Have some. I made the bed. When's the last time you changed the sheets?

JAMIE   Whut's it to ya?

ROSAMUND   I like clean sheets.

JAMIE   Who says you're sleepin' in my bed?

ROSAMUND   I do.
> (JAMIE *approaches her lovingly, then knocks her out*)

JAMIE *(Sings)*
> I never was a courtin' kind of boy
> Them flirtin' games ain't nothin' I enjoy
> I hate a girl to give me goo goo eyes
> If she'd turn her back
> I could sneak attack
> So I git her by surprise

> Cause I like love stolen from the cookie jar
> I like love stolen on the sky—oh yeah!
> I jist love snitchin' what ain't meant for me
> Oh the more forbid
> The sweeter tastes the pie

> A lot of girls are willin' to be had
> The more I see the more it makes me mad
> You grab 'em good—it doesn't faze 'em none
> Well they may be cool
> By the modern rule
> But they're killin' all the fun

Cause I like love stolen from the cookie jar
I like love stolen on the sly—oh yeah!
I jist love snitchin' what ain't meant for me
Oh the more forbid
The sweeter tastes the pie

The more it's prized
The more it's watched oh yeah!
The more it's hid
The more forbid
The sweeter tastes the pie

ROSAMUND   It don't come off.

JAMIE   It never comes off and don't never try to git behind my berrystains cause if you ever do it'll be the end of us.

ROSAMUND   But I want to know whut you look like.

JAMIE   I tole you, the day you see underneath my berrystains is the day we part forever.

ROSAMUND   Yeah, but—whut's yore name?

JAMIE   Unh unh. Less keep it lak we got it with no names. It's more fun. This is the way love oughta be. Like I always wanted it. You here and my wife down there in—

ROSAMUND   Wife?

JAMIE   I bin offered a heiress. Trouble is she's knock-kneed an' cross-eyes an' her brain don't work so right.

ROSAMUND   What're ya marryin' her for?

JAMIE   She's got riches. I'm considerin' this strikly as a bizniss deal. I figger I'll marry with her and love with you.

ROSAMUND   Whut's that make me?

JAMIE   Whut's that make you? That makes you my lover. *(Knocks her out)* I like it like that.

MUSGROVE   Jamie! Jamie!

JAMIE   *(Rushing to remove his disguise and putting on shoes)* Mr. Musgrove, I know it ain't Winsday yet but I been puttin out a lot of inergy lately, thinkin, an' I got happy news. I think it's gonna be jist fine fer me ta marry yer daughter. Jus' lemme avenge her honor with that fiend, won' take me but today an' tomorraw the most, and any time after that is fine for the weddin day. Cain't be too soon fer me. Now where is my luvly bride?

MUSGROVE   Oh God, Jamie, the fiend has stole her away fer good.

SALOME   She's kidnapped. Ain't it awful!

MUSGROVE   I cain't stand it! My baby! But I doan have ta tell you! You luv her as much I do, doancha? Well, if you kin save my baby—yore bride—from the clutches of this monster I'll give you more than her hand. I'll give you half of everythang I own.

SALOME   Clemment!

MUSGROVE   Yore right, wife. It's no time ta be stingy. Jamie, I'll give you everthang I got if you kin git me my girl back.
  (SALOME faints in his arms)

JAMIE Everything! Agreed. I'll find her. By tonight yore girl will be in yore arms.
(HE exits)

MUSGROVE God love you, Jamie Lockhart. We'll be waitin' for ya with the preacher *an the land deed.* Don't take on so much, Salome.

SALOME *(Recovering from faint)* Let me do my grievin' alone, Clemment.

MUSGROVE Cheer up, Salome—we'll get your little girl back for you.
(MUSGROVE exits)

SALOME I got two choices. I can either put a stop to all this or I can throw myself down the well. *(Catches someone's eye)* You shut up! *(Crosses to GOAT, kicks him)* Listen here. . . . The Bandit of the Woods has stole Rosamund away. I want you to go out and find where he's got her hid. Then just come back here, tell me the answer and that sucklin' pig is in yer mama's cook pot.

GOAT I go out in the woods, find out where Rosamund's hid at, come back and tell you . . . and I get a suckling pig. Do you still want a piece of her dress?

SALOME No! Yer mother shudda strangled you at birth. Git!
(GOAT skipping off. LITTLE HARP enters with trunk)

BIG HARP Little Harp! Little Harp! Let me out, brother, I got to talk to you!

LITTLE HARP Shut up! Shut up! I'm sick of tendin' to

you every five minutes. I'm beginning to wonder if you ain't more trouble than you're worth.

BIG HARP   Goddammit! Let me outta here, you dumb jackass.

LITTLE HARP   Quit bein' so cantankerous. What is it this time?

BIG HARP   I been thinkin' about women.

LITTLE HARP   I'm afraid those days are over for you. The Harp Brothers—We were real ladykillers weren't we?

BIG HARP   All we needed was some moonlight and a pretty little lady and a good length of rope.

LITTLE HARP   Remember that preacher's mother up in Port Gibson?

BIG HARP   Couldn't she holler though!

LITTLE HARP   Damn! You got me thinkin' about it. I ain't even seed a woman since before you lost your head.

GOAT   *(Skipping in)*   Suckling pig! Suckling pig! I'm gonna get me a suckling pig!

LITTLE HARP   Sssh! I hear somethin' stupid. I'm gonna git us some dinner from this fool.

GOAT   Hey. How you doing?

LITTLE HARP   How you doing?

GOAT   Fine I reckon.

LITTLE HARP   Good.

GOAT   Unh hunh. I'm gonna git me a sucklin' pig whin I find this beautiful stolen girl.

BIG HARP   Stolen girl?

LITTLE HARP   Whut beautiful stolen girl wuz you referrin' to?

GOAT   Wuz you talkin to that trunk?

LITTLE HARP   No. Tell me about this beautiful stolen girl. Is she young and interestin'?

GOAT   Unh hunh. She's about this tall and she has long yella hair and she runs around the woods nekkid.

BIG HARP   Nekkid?

LITTLE HARP   Nekkid? She does?

GOAT   Unh hunh. Whut's in yer trunk?

LITTLE HARP   Money. Full of money.

GOAT   It smells bad.

LITTLE HARP   Nacherly boy. Money is filthy stuff. If this girl is stolen, she's probably already tied up, ain't she?

GOAT   Unh hunh. I guess so.

LITTLE HARP   Son, can you bring me this tied up, nekkid little—what's her name?

GOAT   Rosamund. Unh unh. A rich lady is givin' me a sucklin' pig for the job.

LITTLE HARP   A sucklin' pig—is that all?
      (Sings)

I'll give you a sack of okra
If you steal me the stolen girl

GOAT *(Sings)*
A sack of okra
Unh hunh
Now who gits to keep the sack?

LITTLE HARP *(Sings)*
You
You git the sack
You git the okra
Fattest little okra barrin' none
And the only thing that I'm gittin'
Is that unfortunate child
Poor tied up darlin'
Poor tied up darlin'
You say she's uhhhhhh?

GOAT *(Sings)*
Uhhhhhh!

LITTLE HARP *(Sings)*
Ahhhhhh?

GOAT *(Sings)*
Ahhhhhh!

LITTLE HARP *(Sings)*
Tell you what I'll do
I'll throw in a bag of butterbeans too
You're gittin' you the beans
And the bag
And the okra
And the sack

And all that I git from you
Is that poor little tied up unfortunate child

You're lookin' a little iffy
So I'll give you my store teeth too

GOAT *(Sings)*
A set of store teeth
Okay
But I got my own right here
See?

LITTLE HARP *(Sings)*
Take home the teeth
They're for your ma
Finest ever made fer dippin' snuff
And the only thing that I'm askin'
Is that su-ufferin' child

BOTH *(Sing)*
Poor tied up darlin'
Poor tied up darlin'

LITTLE HARP *(Sings)*
Has she got uhhhh?

GOAT *(Sings)*
Uhhhh!

LITTLE HARP *(Sings)*
Ahhhh?

GOAT *(Sings)*
Eeeee! ·

LITTLE HARP *(Sings)*
Tell you what I'll do
I'll toss in a cart of chickenshit too

GOAT Chickenshit!

LITTLE HARP *(Sings)*
> You git the shit
> And the cart
> And the teeth for yer ma
> And the beans
> And the bag
> And the okra
> And the sack
> And all I got from you
> Is that poor little put upon tied up unfortunate
>   child

> Wait!
> I'll give you a jew's harp
> Roof tarp
> How's about a sickle sharp
> Plus a pair of cupboard doors
> A pair of winter underdrawers
> A wooden leg
> A rutabega
> Keg of corn to keep you drunk

GOAT *(Sings)*
> An' everthang thass in yer trunk

LITTLE HARP *(Sings)*
> My trunk?

GOAT *(Sings)*
> All I want is all thass in yer trunk
> Deal?

LITTLE HARP *(Sings)*
> Deal!

BOTH *(Sing)*
> Poor tied up darlin!
> Poor tied up darlin!
> Oh yes she's bound and gagged
> And drugged and bagged
> That pitiful dear
> Is comin' here
> And
> Oh Lordy
> Lordy
> Don't it make you git a heartache!

LITTLE HARP   All right. It's a bargain. If you don't live up to it, boy, I'll beat you to a pulp like I did Jamie Lockhart over at the inn in Rodney and there wasn't nothin left of him but the juice. You understand? All right then. I'll meet you right here. You and the pore disabled young lady.

BIG HARP   You're a fine brother! Tradin' me away like a plug of tobacca.

LITTLE HARP   Shut up. Where is that fool boy?

BIG HARP   And you always sayin'
> *(Sung)*
> Two heads are better than one.

LITTLE HARP   I don't need you no more, Big Harp. This little nekkid Rosamund has a head, don't she? Plus a few little extras you ain't never had.

GOAT *(To the* GROUP*)*   I'm gonna be rich! Uh oh. What if I cain't find Rosamund? Hey, I got an idea. I'll take him my unmarried sister, Airie. He'll never know the difference. Airie! Airie!

(GOAT *goes to get* AIRIE *in the sack.* GOAT *enters with*
AIRIE *in sack*)

LITTLE HARP   You done it! You done it, boy! Oh my,
she looks pathetic.

GOAT   You can have her on one condition.

LITTLE HARP   Whut?

GOAT   You got to marry her.

LITTLE HARP   Course. Course I will. Done said agreed.
Here's your trunk. (GOAT *starts to open it*) No wait!
Don't open it yet. It's not ready to be opened—
    (*But it's too late.* GOAT *has opened the trunk and pulls
    out* BIG HARP)

BIG HARP   What the hell are you looking at?

GOAT (*Delighted*)   A head? A head? Why didn't you tell
me? This is better than money.

LITTLE HARP   It is?

GOAT   Unh hunh. My mamma always says.

GOAT'S MOTHER'S VOICE   Goat, every day I pray you'll
come home with a good head on your shoulders.

GOAT   I'm gonna take you home with me.

BIG HARP and GOAT   Bye!
    (GOAT *takes the trunk off*)

LITTLE HARP   Hello in there, little miss nekkid! (*Pokes at
bag with his knife*) We're fixin' to have us some fun!
Rosamund! Rosamund!
    (AIRIE *screams in the sack*)

JAMIE *(With his face half stained)*   Success! There's my heiress. Afternoon, Little Harp.

LITTLE HARP   Well, if it ain't the Bandit of the Woods.

JAMIE   Whut you got there?

LITTLE HARP   Well, I fin'ly got me a wife.

JAMIE   Why you got her in a sack?

LITTLE HARP   I bought her sight unseen and test untested. I figured she must be in demand. *(*AIRIE *screams. To* AIRIE *very threatening)* Shut up, or I'll take my knife an' slice you up the center.

JAMIE   Game's over, Little Harp. This girl belongs to me. She's mine.

LITTLE HARP   No she ain't. No she ain't. I bargained fair and square with that halfwit and I gave him my—leggo you sunuvabitch. *(Frightened)* Oh, Lordy! You're the ghost of Jamie Lockhart! And you're the Bandit of the Woods too! You got yore two faces on and I see both of you.

JAMIE   Oh my God. God all mighty. I'm gonna hafta kill you.

LITTLE HARP   No you ain't. Hell, where's my knife? You ain't no ghost. You tricked me. You tricked me.

JAMIE   —hell, you ain't worth stickin. *(Knocks him out)* That'll take care of you till I git back. Come on, Miss Musgrove. Let's us go and git married. Where'd she go?
       *(*ENSEMBLE *points in different directions.* JAMIE *exits)*

SALOME *(To the* GROUP*)*   I think I conjured up where she is! Somethin' tells me Rosamund is livin' like a queen yonder in them woods with that bandit. But things are fixin' ta change.

THE RAVEN *(Calls)*
Mean as a snake
Still as a mouse
Trouble's comin' up
To Rosamund's house

Crawley like a ant
Black like a crow
Trouble's comin' up fer her an' her beau

Git away Rosamund
Git away quick
Trouble's comin' to ya good an' thick
     (ROSAMUND *is in her house.* SALOME *approaches)*

SALOME   Rosamund! Rosamund! Surprise!

ROSAMUND *(Belligerent)*   Stepmother, I ain' leavin'. You cain' make me do it!

SALOME   Who sed anything about leavin'? I jist come fer a visit. Look what I brung ya!

ROSAMUND   Unh hunh. I guess Daddy knows where I am too!

SALOME   Quit ditherin', sugar. You thank I want you back home? Whut fer whin I bin tryin' to git rid of you since I got there?

ROSAMUND   Whut do you want thin?

SALOME (Barbara Land) and ROSAMUND (Rhonda Coullet), the Broadway production.

SALOME I come to make sure yer here permanent. (ROSAMUND *accepts this*) Is he good to you?

ROSAMUND Oh yes! The Bandit of the Woods is a wonderful provider! Ev'ry day he robs a traisure for me and brings it home and ev'ry night there is no end to our joy.

SALOME *(Boiling with jealousy)* My goodness, honey! You sound so happy! *(Crafty)* I notice you call him the Bandit of the Woods. Whut's his name?

ROSAMUND I—promised not to tell.

SALOME I see. Well, whut duz he look like?

ROSAMUND I—I'm not supposed to tell you that.

SALOME Rosamund, this is yer stepmother, Salome, talkin'. You ain't foolin' me. You doan know his name, do ya? You never seen his face.

ROSAMUND He never takes the berrystains off.

SALOME Rosamund, how kin you love a man that woan even do you the common courtesy of lettin' you see his face?

ROSAMUND I—

SALOME Doan you want to know whut he looks like? Jist a little peek?

ROSAMUND The Bandit of the Woods tole me if I ever saw beneath his stains it would be the end of us.

SALOME Sugar baby, let me help you.

ROSAMUND You kin?

SALOME Well, I happen to have a pefickly wonderful recipe fer removin' berrystains.

ROSAMUND You do!—But he said—

SALOME Oh thass jist talk. Now, git you three fresh duck eggs. Break 'em in clear rain water. Stir it up. But not too much. Add a pincha red pepper, some saffron, a little rue and pore in a pint jar of plum vinegar. Churn it up and down till it foams, rub it on easy like and them stains'll cum right off. It can't fail.

ROSAMUND Did you say sage?

SALOME No, saffron, sugar. And duck eggs. Seems to me I saw a duck settin' on a nest over by the pond on my way here.

ROSAMUND Stepmother— Why have we always bin such enemies?

SALOME I doan know. Waste a' energy, wadn't it? Rosamund, I'd lak you ta call me mother.

ROSAMUND Thank you—mother.

SALOME Now you better git and find them duck eggs! (ROSAMUND *exits*) Thank you, Mother! (*To the* COMPANY) I always knew she's dumb lak her Daddy. She's gonna take them berrystains off the Bandit of the Woods an' he'll run out on her! Maybe he'll smash her, and I woan have to thank about that snippy thing again. (SHE *sings happily as* LITTLE HARP *approaches the house*)

LITTLE HARP This here's Jamie Lockhart's house! He got my girl and now I'm gonna git his. I'm gonna do worse than git her. I'm gonna put Jamie Lockhart's girl in this sack here and throw her inta th' ravine.

THE RAVEN   Turn back, my bonny. Turn away home!

LITTLE HARP   You're some fine feathered friend, aincha? Nobody flies out on Little Harp! (HE *strangles the* RA-VEN. *To the* COMPANY) Git this dead bird outta here. Well, that must be the girl. I hear she's young and juicy. (*To* SALOME *from outside the robber's house*) Hay there, young an' juicy!
(Pause)

SALOME   Hay there, yourself. (LITTLE HARP *enters. Sees* LITTLE HARP, *dismayed*) Are you the Bandit of the Woods?

LITTLE HARP *(To the* GROUP*)*   Are you Jamie Lockhart's girl? Lord, he's got peculiar taste! This is Jamie Lockhart's house, ain't it?

SALOME   It ain't. This is whar the Bandit of the Woods lives. Git goin'.

LITTLE HARP   This is the place thin. You cain't fool me. I saw two faces sitting on the same man's head and I know that the Bandit of the Woods and Jamie Lockhart are wun and the same person.

SALOME   How do you know that?

LITTLE HARP   I seen. I seen the bandit with his stains off and it's Jamie Lockhart underneath.

SALOME   Well. Jamie Lockhart is the Bandit uv the Woods. Whut you want?

LITTLE HARP   I want his girl.

SALOME Whut fer?

LITTLE HARP (*Shaking his sack*) Jamie—sint me fer her.

SALOME Whut fer?

LITTLE HARP He—wants to make love to her out in the woods!

SALOME He does? Well!

LITTLE HARP Unh hunh. On a pine needle floor, he said, with nobody but the bugs an' the birds to see whut happins.

SALOME I'm the girl yer lookin' for.

LITTLE HARP You sure? I doan wanna make no mistakes.

SALOME Course I'm sure. Ain't I livin' here in his house?

LITTLE HARP You sure? I doan wanna make no mistakes.

SALOME In this sack?

LITTLE HARP That wuz his orders an' thass the way he hopes ta see his loverlady. He's waitin' for you in the woods now pawin' the ground.

SALOME I'm comin'. I'm comin'. I'm comin'.

COMPANY (*Sings*)
    Goodbye Salome
    Goodbye you lucky lady
    Off you go to paradise
    Git set Salome
    Yer headin' right fer heaven
    Times like this doan happen twice

I got the feelin'
Yore gonna fly
Yore gonna raise up off the ground an' float away
I got the feelin' it's in the bag
You're gonna fin'ly git whut you deserve today
Dress up Salome
Yore goin' off ta glory
The big event is near
Dress up Salome
Git set Salome
Goodbye Salome dear
Sing oh sing my joyful heart
Soon Salome will depart
Luck will fall in her lap
She's goin' off in burlap
And if my happiness is showin'
It's 'cause I know jist whare she's goin'
Goodbye Salome
Goodbye you lucky lady
Off you go to paradise
Git set Salome
Yore heading right fer heaven
Times lak this doan happen twice
I got the feelin' yore gonna fly
You're gonna raise up off the ground an' float away
I got the feelin' it's in the bag
Yore gonna fin'ly git whut you deserve today
Fix up Salome
Yer goin' off ta glory
The big event is near
Dress up Salome
Git set Salome
Goodbye Salome dear

Dress up Salome
Git set Salome
Goodbye Salome dear
Dress up Salome
Git set Salome
Goodbye, goodbye, goodbye, goodbye
Salome dear
(SALOME *gets in the sack and* LITTLE HARP *throws the sack into the ravine*)

ROSAMUND *(After "Goodbye Salome")* I hope I'm doin the right thang messing around with them berrystains. Mother, Stepmother, Salome, I made your stain re—who are you?

LITTLE HARP I—Damn! I thank I made a mistake.

ROSAMUND Git outta here.

LITTLE HARP Unh unh. An' this is gonna be more fun than the other wun 'cause you are pretty lak they said.

ROSAMUND Quit ticklin' me! (HE *is on top of her.* JAMIE *rushes in, pulls his knife and stabs* LITTLE HARP)

LITTLE HARP Damn! (HE *dies*)

JAMIE Evenin'.

ROSAMUND Evenin'. You look poorly!

JAMIE I never killed nobody before. Nuthin' went right today. I lost my heiress.

ROSAMUND Yer precious lame brain. Thass a giant pity.

JAMIE I cain't find her anywhere . . .

ROSAMUND   Yore heart must be broke into cake crumbs over it.

JAMIE   I want them riches, fer you an' me.

ROSAMUND *(Remembering the jug)*   Lissen, you cain' do innything now. You got time fer a little nap before dinner.

JAMIE   I doan need no nap.

ROSAMUND   Sure you do. Come on. Make you feel better.
(Sings)
Been a busy day
With some heavy seas
But you done your best
Sleepy man
Let your troubles lay
Let your breathin' ease
While I rub your chest
Sleepy man

You're all done with the run of the race for today
You got plenty of runnin' to face come tomorrow
I'm right here
Always near
Always lovin' my dear sleepy man

Not a girl I know
Has a better deal
Than my life with you
Sleepy man
If I let it show
How you make me feel

We'll be up till two
Sleepy man

And you're done with the run of the race for today
You got plenty of runnin' to face come tomorrow
I'm right here
Always near
Always lovin' my dear sleepy man

I'm right here
Always near
And I love you my dear sleepy man
        (Having removed the berrystains)
I'll be damned. Jamie Lockhart. Hey, wake up.

JAMIE Huh? Dinner ready?

ROSAMUND You wuz sayin' your little heiress wuz kid-napped?

JAMIE Thass right. Whut'd you wake me up fer?

ROSAMUND I, uh, found her fore you.

JAMIE You did? Don't fool with me. *(Goes back to sleep.*
ROSAMUND *dishevels herself as* SHE *was under the table)*

ROSAMUND Well, thank you for the hairpins, Mr. Jamie
Lockhart!
        *(*SHE *sings)*
If you don't come kiss me I'll run like a turkey!
        *(*HE *sits bolt upright)*

JAMIE No! You? My heiress? *(*SHE *nods, pleased)* You
really messed things up now.

ROSAMUND Messed up! Oh no! Jist take me back to
Daddy. I know he'll give you a good reward. He's

real ginerous! And we kin git married an' live richer than you ever dreamed of.

JAMIE   You had to ruin everthang, didn' ya? Musgrove's daughter! Oh damn!

ROSAMUND   Don't you want to marry me?

JAMIE   Of course I don't. I want to love you. Marriage is bizness. I never mix bizness with love.

ROSAMUND   Love! With no names! And those damn stains on yer face! You don' want love. You want a little something to git you thru the night. Well, not from me no more. I'm goin' home.

JAMIE   Good. Fine. Go. Git out. Don't be here whin I git back.

ROSAMUND   I wouldn't stay here for the second coming. (JAMIE *leaves*) He's jist a robber. I wanted a bridegroom. He never called a damn thang by its true name, even his name or mine. And whut I wanted ta give him he ruther steal frum me. I hate him. I love him. Oh God, I got ta find him! I got ta find Jamie Lockhart!
    (SHE *runs out.* JAMIE *returns to the house*)

JAMIE   I changed my mind! Hey! Rosamund! Rosamund! I never said her name before. It's nice. Rosamund! Rosamund! She's gone. She's gone.
    (JAMIE *enters looking for* ROSAMUND. *Pause.* HE *looks all through the* COMPANY. *Sings*)
    I could die
    Just like a poor stepped on fly
    I could shrivel up and die

From my sorrow—from my deep sorrow
Where oh where oh where is my baby darlin'?
Where oh where oh where is my baby darlin'?
Rosamund!
   (Echo—"Rosamund")
Rosamund! Jamie!

MUSGROVE *(Sings)*
Baby love
Have you been took up above
Did you shrivel up and die
Oh my sorrow—oh my deep deep sorrow
Where oh where oh where is my baby darlin'?
Where oh where oh where is my baby darlin'?

JAMIE *(At the same time, sings)*
Let me die
Let me shrivel up and die
Don't care how hard I try
I can't find her—why?
Where oh where oh where is my baby darlin'?
Where oh where oh where is my baby darlin'?

There she is behind the pine tree
No, it's just the tail of a movin' redbird
Everywhere I swear I see her
Losin' her has made me lose my mind

ROSAMUND *(Sings)*
Where oh where is my Jamie Lockhart?

MUSGROVE *(Sings)*
Where oh where is my baby darlin'?

JAMIE *(Sings)*
Rosamund! Damn it!

ROSAMUND *(Sings)*
> Where is he?
> I looked from here to Tennessee
> I could shrivel up and die
> From my sorrow—from my deep deep sorrow
> Where oh where oh where is my Jamie darlin'?
> Where oh where oh where is my Jamie darlin'?
> Jamie Lockhart!   Jamie Lockhart!

JAMIE *(At the same time, sings)*
> Let me die
> Shrivel up and die
> From my sorrow—deep deep sorrow
> Oh where oh where oh where is my baby darlin'?
> Where oh where oh where is my baby darlin'?
> Rosamund!   Rosamund!

MUSGROVE *(At the same time, sings)*
> Baby love
> You must be deep in the ground in the grave
> Lordy, where oh where oh where is my baby
>   darlin'?
> Where oh where oh where is my baby darlin'?
> Rosamund! Rosamund!

TOWNSPEOPLE *(At the same time, sing)*
> Rosamund
> Jamie Lockhart
> Rosamund
> Jamie Lockhart
> Rosamund
> Jamie Lockhart
> Rosamund
> Jamie Lockhart

Where oh where oh where is my baby darlin'?
Where oh where oh where is my baby darlin'?

Rosamund
Jamie Lockhart

JAMIE *(Sings)*
My poor little baby darlin'.
She's gone! I'll never see Rosamund again. It must
have been in the stars.

A MAN Where are you going?

JAMIE Well, I'm going where beauty and vice and
every delight possible to the soul and body wait in the
doorways and bloom beneath every palmetto, where
the very atmosphere is aerial spice. The walls are
sugar cane and the clouds hang golden as bananas in
the sky. I'm going to New Orleans. Why not? I'm
still Jamie Lockhart, aren't I?
(Exits. GOAT *enters, takes top of barrel.* ROSAMUND
sticks her head up)

GOAT Hey, how're you doin'?

ROSAMUND Who are you?

GOAT Name's Goat. I work for your stepmama.

ROSAMUND I b'leve it. Have you seen Jamie Lockhart
anywhere?

GOAT Jamie Lockhart the ghost?

ROSAMUND My God! Is he a ghost now?

GOAT Unh hunh. Little Harp told me he whacked his
brains out at the inn in Rodney with a piece of the

floor. Wadn' nothing left of Jamie Lockhart but the juice, he said.

ROSAMUND   When was that?

GOAT   I'd say nine months ago.

ROSAMUND *(Revealing stomach)*   Nine months—thass interestin'.

A WOMAN   Well, if he is a ghost, I seen it the other day. It was runnin' a big drygoods store.

ROSAMUND   My God! Where?

THE WOMAN   On Royale Street in New Orleans.

ROSAMUND   I got ta find it. That ghost is the father of my baby!

GOAT   I'll take you down the Natchez Trace. All the way to New Orleans.

TOWNSPEOPLE *(Call)*
    Pass her along—she's nearabout a mother
    Pass her along—she's nearabout a mother
    Pass her along—she's nearabout a mother
    Don't nobody rob her

A BANDIT   Drop that treasure.

TOWNSPEOPLE *(Call)*
    See that belly there? Handle her with care
    Pass her along—she's nearabout a mother

ANOTHER BANDIT   Stick 'em up, Fatso.

TOWNSPEOPLE *(Call)*
    Can't you see she's nearabout a mother

ANOTHER BANDIT *(Calls)*   Course I see she's nearabout a
  mother

TOWNSPEOPLE *(Call)*
  Then pass her to New Orleans
  Pass her along—she's nearabout a mother

ANOTHER BANDIT   Stand and deliver.

GOAT   Oh, Mister, I think you said the wrong thing.
  *(ROSAMUND groans with labor pains. A quilt is held
  up. Behind it ROSAMUND has twins)*

A SHIP CAPTAIN   All aboard for a upriver voyage ta
  Rodney's Landing.

JAMIE *(Coming through the CROWD)*   I'm comin', Captain.
  Hold the ship.

ROSAMUND   Jamie Lockhart! I found you!

JAMIE   Rosamund! Oh Rosamund! Oh Lord!
  (JAMIE spins, sees ROSAMUND and the babies)

ROSAMUND   This is Clemmentine and Jamie Junior.
  (THEY bend down to kiss)

JAMIE   Success! Preacher!

A CALLER
  Find a partner—swing fer yer life
  Make this couple man and wife

  Proper is as proper does
  Better late than never was

  Walk yore partner back and fore
  While they promise evermore

Stroll yer corner straight ahead
Okay people—they are wed

Pass their children down the line
Hold 'em tight and treat 'em fine

Whin yer married time goes fast
Lord! A whole long year has passed
Face yer mate and give a bow
Look who's in New Orleans now
Ain't New Orleans fine and rare
Pssst! Mr. Musgrove! Look athere!

MUSGROVE Baby! Is it you?

ROSAMUND Daddy! Daddy! Oh, Daddy, don't cry! We're all right. Jamie and me are married now.

MUSGROVE Well. Look at that. I thought I'd never see you again. But you're married to a bandit.

JAMIE I'm a merchant now, Mr. Musgrove. I steal with style.

ROSAMUND We got a fine house right on Lake Pontchatrain. Marble and cypress and our bed has a sky blue silk canopy floating over it and I own eighty-four dresses.

MUSGROVE Baby, is this really true?

ROSAMUND Of course, Daddy.

JAMIE All but the blue canopy.

ROSAMUND Stay with us, Daddy.

MUSGROVE No. I better git on up to the plantation. I doan belong here. (To JAMIE) Take this, son.

JAMIE   I got plinty of money now.

MUSGROVE   Buy my baby that blue canopy she wants. Say it's frum me.

CAPTAIN   All aboard!

MUSGROVE   *(Moving on to boat)*   Oh, there's my boat sugar pie. I guess I got to get on board. Take care of yourself, Baby.

ROSAMUND   I will, Daddy, I promise. But we didn't even get a chance to talk about anything. I want to know about home. Hey, Daddy, how's Salome?

MUSGROVE   Oh, she's fine. She's dead. Bye.
        (The boat moves off)

NARRATOR   *(Calls)*
        Move along and grab some one
        Robber Bridegroom tale is done
        Eat yore quail an' sip yore wine
        Jamie Lockhart's doin' fine
        Circle round and gather right
        Okay neighbors end it right

ENSEMBLE   *(Sings)*
        We never would stand here and lie in your face
        That's exactly how it happened
        Once upon the Natchez Trace

        We never would stand here and lie in your face
        That's exactly how it happened

JAMIE   *(Sings)*
        A gent and a robber all in one

ROSAMUND *(Sings)*
  A girl who made the moon burn like the sun

SALOME *(Sings)*
  A greedy witch

MUSGROVE *(Sings)*
  A man that rich

GOAT *(Sings)*
  A brain that big

LITTLE HARP *(Sings)*
  A filthy pig

BIG HARP *(Sings)*
  A talking head

JAMIE *(Sings)*
  And as I said
  A hell of a lot happened around here.

ALL *(Sing)*
  Once upon the Natchez Trace
  Once upon the Natchez Trace

CURTAIN